Mom, Cheers to You!

by
Lucinda Roberts

Cre.Alli Publishing House

Unless otherwise indicated all Scripture quotations are taken from the *King James Version* of the Bible.

Front cover stock image: krupenikova.olga/Shutterstock.com

Published by Cre.Alli Publishing House
Balch Springs, TX 75181

Copyright © 2025 by Lucinda Roberts

All rights reserved.

ISBN 979-8998587009

No portion of this book may be reproduced, distributed or transmitted in any form without written permission from the publisher or author, except as permitted by U.S. copyright law.

Dedication

To my Mother

Contents

Introduction
1   Memories & Special Moments
2   A Few of Your Favorite Things
3   Gratitude & Love
4   Favorite Traditions & Shared Experiences
5   Looking Ahead & Legacy

Introduction

Now, who is this book for?
It's for mothers, daughters, and sons.

It's for anyone who feels that tug at their heart, knowing they want to deepen their connection with their mom. Whether you're close as can be or miles apart, this book is for you.

Expressing love and appreciation has a profound emotional impact. It can transform your relationship, bringing you closer and creating lasting memories. When we make it a habit to show our love, we open the door to deeper understanding and connection.

So, I invite you to take this journey. Engage with this living tribute to your mom, dive into the exercises and prompts, and make it a project of love. Let's start this new phase of love and connection together. Your mom deserves to know how you feel, and you deserve the joy of telling her.

Mom, Cheers to You!

...just because

1
Memories & Special Moments

Memories & Special Moments

Mom, one of my earliest memories of you is...

Mom, Cheers to You!

I'll never forget the time you made me feel especially loved when...

Memories & Special Moments

The little things you did, like

_____,

made a big difference in my life because...

Mom, Cheers to You!

When I was going through a tough time, you were there for me by...

Memories & Special Moments

Your love has shaped me into the person I am today by...

Mom, Cheers to You!

If I could make sure you knew just one thing, it would be...

Memories & Special Moments

Mom, Cheers to You!

"God's divine power has given us everything we need for life and for godliness. This power was given to us through knowledge of the One who called us by His own glory and integrity."
2 Peter 1:3 GOD'S WORD® Translation

Memories & Special Moments

In every challenge and every triumph, His strength shines through you. Even when the road seems long or the days feel heavy, you're empowered by a love that never quits. You are never alone and all you have is all you need. Christ's strength lives in you, lifting you up and propelling you forward and upward, no matter the obstacle. Let this truth remind you that you can overcome anything with His grace guiding you every step of the way

Mom, Cheers to You!

Memories & Special Moments

Mom, Cheers to You!

"I praise you, for I am fearfully and wonderfully made. Wonderful are your works; my soul knows it very well. "
Psalm 139:14 KJV

Memories & Special Moments

Be reminded of the beauty and wonder that God has woven into every part of us. Just as He created the world with careful intention, He created you with love and precision. You are a unique masterpiece, crafted with strength, grace, and endless beauty.

May you always see in yourself the wonder that others so admire. I'm so grateful for the amazing person you are and the light you bring into my life.

Mom, Cheers to You!

2

A Few of Your Favorite Things...

Mom, Cheers to You!

Mom, I always remember how much you loved (favorite food),

_____

and it makes me think of you when...

A Few of Your Favorite Things

Your favorite saying was always

_____

,
and I find myself repeating it when

Mom, Cheers to You!

You always had a way of saying

_____

that made me smile because...

A Few of Your Favorite Things

One of the songs you loved most was

_____,

and every time I hear it, I…

Mom, Cheers to You!

I can still picture you enjoying (favorite activity/hobby),

_____

and I loved watching you...

A Few of Your Favorite Things

Mom, Cheers to You!

"Be still, and know that I am God"
Psalm 46:10 (ESV)

A Few of Your Favorite Things

When your day feels overwhelming, take a pause and let your heart rest.
God is inviting you into a sanctuary of peace, where every burden is lifted and every hope is renewed. Allow His love to work wonders in those quiet moments, filling your life with unexpected grace and clarity.
Always remember how truly treasured you are.

Mom, Cheers to You!

A Few of Your Favorite Things

Mom, Cheers to You!

"God is within her, she will not fall;
God will help her at break of day."
Psalms 46:5 (NIV)

A Few of Your Favorite Things

God's strength is right there in you. With His presence, you stand firm each new day through every challenge. Know that since God cannot fail, once He is inside you, you are assured of victory over every situation and circumstance of life. His help lifts you up. Even on the toughest mornings, His love renews your strength. Always remember that you are a beacon of resilience and grace—cherished beyond measure.

Mom, Cheers to You!

3
Gratitude & Love

Mom, Cheers to You!

I just want to say thank you for...

Gratitude & Love

Now that I'm older, I can see how much you sacrificed when you…

Mom, Cheers to You!

One of the things I admire most about you is...

Gratitude & Love

Your love has shaped me into the person I am today by...

Mom, Cheers to You!

One thing I didn't understand about you when I was growing up that I do now is....

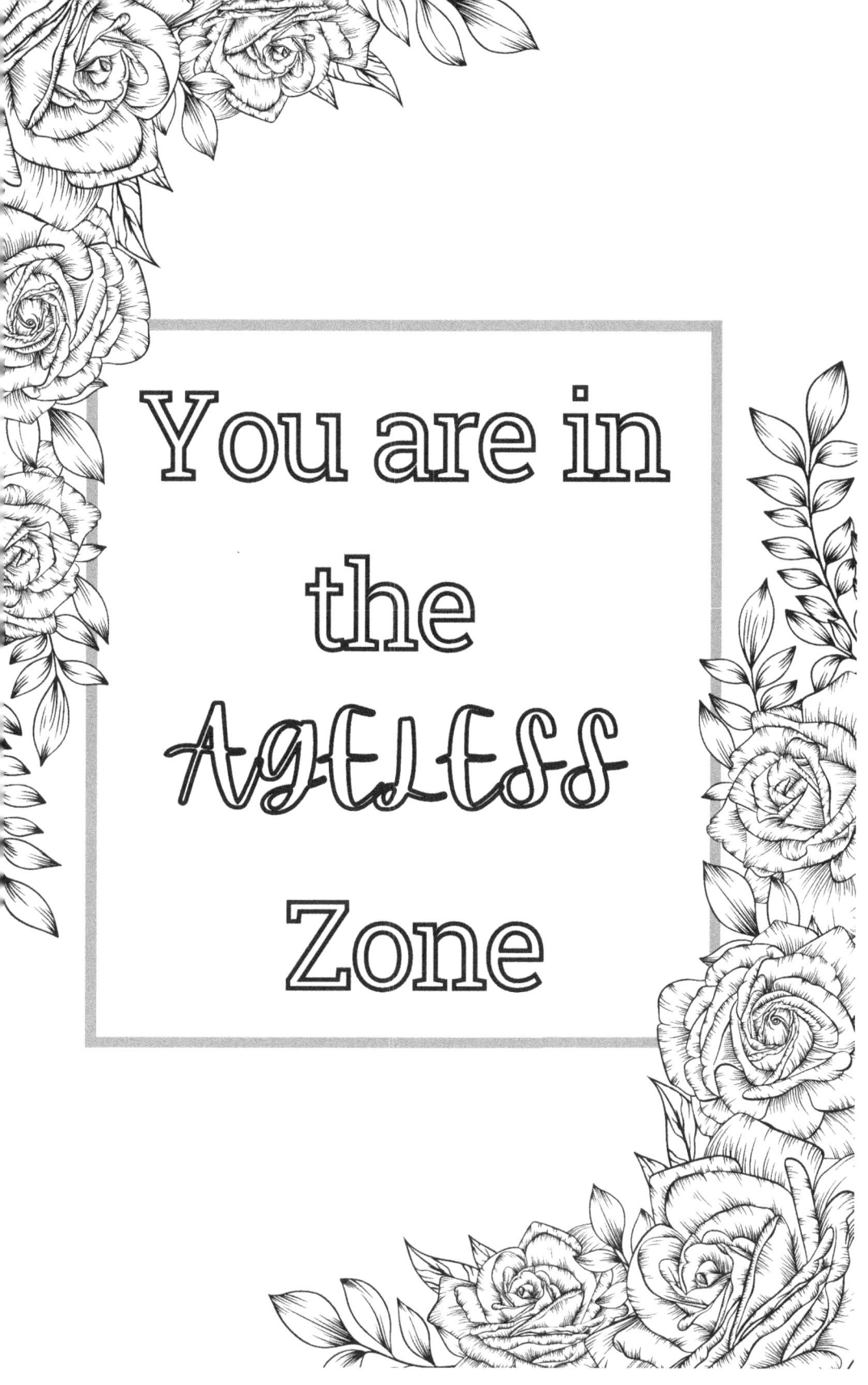

Gratitude & Love

THOUGHTS

Mom, Cheers to You!

"Bless the Lord, O my soul...Who satisfies your years with good things, So that your youth is renewed like the [soaring] eagle. Psalm 103:4,5 AMP

Gratitude & Love

Years come and years go , but, God's love keeps you forever young. He fills your life with blessings that make each day a fresh start, renewing your spirit and preserving your ageless beauty. Like the soaring eagle, your strength and vitality rise above time, proving that true youth comes from the grace that sustains you.

May you always feel the wonder of His enduring care, keeping you vibrant and ever-renewed.

Mom, Cheers to You!

Gratitude & Love

Mom, Cheers to You!

"For everything there is a season, and a time for every matter under heaven:"
Ecclesiastes 3:1 ESV

Gratitude & Love

Seasons!

Through the cycles of life, take hold of the beauty of each moment, knowing that every experience has shaped you into the incredible mother you are.

In times of joy, you dance with abandon; in times of sorrow, you allow yourself to heal. You are a master gardener, planting seeds of love and nurturing them with grace to produce a bountiful harvest. Trust the process, for every season has its purpose. The Lord is with you in every transition, guiding you from glory to glory. It's harvest now...look up and see the blessings that even now are overflowing in your life and the lives of those you love!

Mom, Cheers to You!

4
Favorite Traditions & Shared Experiences

Mom, Cheers to You!

One of my favorite things we always did together was...

Favorite Traditions & Shared Experiences

Every time I hear (or smell/taste/see)

_____,

it reminds me of you because...

Mom, Cheers to You!

One of my favorite memories of us is the time we...

Favorite Traditions & Shared Experiences

One of the greatest lessons you ever taught me was...

Mom, Cheers to You!

If I could relive one day of my childhood with you, it would be the day we...

Favorite Traditions & Shared Experiences

My favorite celebration with you was...

Mom, Cheers to You!

Mom, Cheers to You!

Favorite Traditions & Shared Experiences

Mom, Cheers to You!

"And the LORD will guide you continually and satisfy your desire in scorched places and make your bones strong; and you shall be like a watered garden, like a spring of water, whose waters do not fail."
Isaiah 58:11 ESV

Favorite Traditions & Shared Experiences

The Lord has promised never to leave you or forsake you. He is your constant companion, the Friend who sticks closer than a brother, guiding you through every hardship and satisfying your deepest longings. He constantly refreshes your spirit and fortifies your heart, making you a vibrant oasis, overflowing with His love and grace.

Embrace His guidance, for He has ushered you into a season of growth and abundance. You are a source of life, a spring that never runs dry. Get ready to experience His goodness in ways that will leave you in awe! Get ready to witness His miraculous provision!

Mom, Cheers to You!

Favorite Traditions & Shared Experiences

Mom, Cheers to You!

"Never doubt God's mighty power to work in you and accomplish all this. He will achieve infinitely more than your greatest request, your most unbelievable dream, and exceed your wildest imagination! He will outdo them all, for his miraculous power constantly energizes you." Ephesians 3:20 TPT

Favorite Traditions & Shared Experiences

It's time to dream big! As you take those steps of faith, God will work wonders in your life, surpassing every expectation you hold. You live above the systems of the world and are filled with His miraculous energy. He will bring your dreams to fruition in ways that will astound you. Trust in His greatness, for He is about to do something incredible in your life!

Mom, Cheers to You!

Mom, Cheers to You!

5
Looking Ahead & Legacy

Mom, Cheers to You!

I wish you could truly know just how much you have meant to me because...

Looking Ahead & Legacy

I will always honor your memory by...

Mom, Cheers to You!

No matter what, I will always carry

_____

in my heart because of you.

Looking Ahead & Legacy

I see your influence in my life today when I…

Mom, Cheers to You!

Most of all, I want you to know...

Mom, Cheers to You!

Looking Ahead & Legacy

THOUGHTS

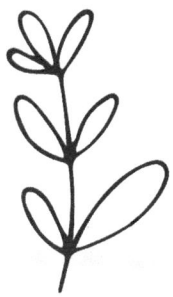

Mom, Cheers to You!

"Now, may the grace and joyous favor of the Lord Jesus Christ, the unambiguous love of God, and the precious communion that we share in the Holy Spirit be yours continually. Amen!"
2 Corinthians 13:14 TPT

Mom, Cheers to You!

Your feedback is greatly appreciated!

It's through your feedback, support and reviews that we're able to create the best books possible and serve more people.

We would be extremely grateful if you could take just 60 seconds to kindly leave an honest review of the book on Amazon. Please share your feedback and thoughts for others to see.

To do so, simply find the book on Amazon's website (or wherever you purchased the book from) and locate the section to leave a review. Select a star rating and write a couple of sentences.

That's it! Thank you so much for your support.

Review this product

Share your thoughts with other customers

Write a customer review

Made in the USA
Coppell, TX
25 April 2025

48655727R00066